Pickling & Preserves
ORGANIZER

CICO BOOKS
LONDON NEW YORK

Published in 2010 by CICO Books
An imprint of Ryland Peters & Small Ltd
20–21 Jockey's Fields   519 Broadway, 5th Floor
London WC1R 4BW   New York, NY 10012

www.cicobooks.com

10 9 8 7 6 5 4 3 2 1

Text copyright © Gloria Nicol and CICO Books 2010
Design and photography © CICO Books 2010

The authors' moral rights have been asserted. All rights reserved. No part of this publication may be reproduced, stored in a retrieval system, or transmitted in any form or by any means, electronic, mechanical, photocopying, or otherwise, without the prior permission of the publisher.

A CIP catalog record for this book is available from the Library of Congress and the British Library.

ISBN-13: 978 1 907030 78 9

Printed in China

Editor: Pete Jorgensen
Text: Gloria Nicol
Designer: Roger Hammond at Blue Gum Designers
Illustrators: Fahema Khanam and Jane Smith
See page 128 for picture credits

Contents

Introduction: **Getting started**
Preserving equipment 7
Preserving techniques 10

1. Jams & jellies
Strawberry & vanilla jam 20
Cherry jam 22
Blackberry jelly 23
Raspberry jelly 23
White currant & red chili jam 24
Record pages 25

2. Curds & marmalades
Lemon curd 49
Bitter orange curd 49
Seville orange marmalade 50
Peach marmalade 51
Butternut & ginger curd 52
Record pages 53

3. Chutneys & pickles
Mango chutney 74
Pumpkin chutney 76
Pickled shallots 77
Green tomato & red onion chutney 78
Record pages 79

4. Nectars & cordials
Ginger & lemon nectar 103
Lemon & orange nectar 103
Figs in vanilla syrup 104
Apricots in syrup 105
Raspberry nectar 106
Record pages 107

Notes 122
Favorite websites 126
Useful contacts & picture credits 128

Introduction:

Getting started

Whatever your tastes, there is certain to be a pickle or a preserve to suit you. The choices of recipes are endless, and you will be sure to find a delicious condiment that will use up some of the produce you have grown yourself. Making them is straight-forward as well, and this section explains all the elements that go into producing your own jams, chutneys, curds, and more.

If this is your first attempt at making a marmalade or a cordial then this section will guide you through all the information you need to know, from understanding the pectin content of fruit to making your own pickling vinegar. And even if you are an old hand at making your own jellies and nectars, you should find some helpful tips that will improve your end results.

Choosing your ingredients

Although strawberries—to give just one example—can now be bought virtually all year round, thanks to the introduction of new varieties, the use of field tunnels, and the increase in imported produce, nothing beats the flavor of a sun-ripened, homegrown strawberry that has been picked only moments before. It is this intense, sweet flavor that can be captured in preserves.

Using your own homegrown produce for preserving is hard to beat, because the ingredients will be fresh and you will have control over their growing conditions.

Farmers' markets are another great source. You'll know that the fruit and vegetables have been grown locally, and you are more likely to find unusual varieties. Whatever its source, rinse produce before use, although ideally not bush fruits since rinsing can reduce their juice content. However, if they may have been sprayed, you will need to rinse and drain them.

Food for free

Ingredients are often right in front of your nose, all you have to do is find them. Woodlands and hedgerows (if you live in an area where these are common) are full of edible fruits and berries if you know what to look for. Crab apples often grow wild, as do greengages, damsons, or blackberries. Alternatively, if you know someone who grows more fruit than they can use, offer to take some in exchange for a jar of preserve made using it. It's a win-win situation.

Fruit and pectin

For almost all fruit preserves you need to choose fresh, good-quality, just-ripe fruit in order to achieve the correct pectin content.

This is because jam needs the right balance of pectin, acid, and sugar to set properly. Different fruits contain varying amounts of pectin, and the pectin content is higher in just-ripe fruit. Crab apples, Seville oranges, damsons, quinces, and currants are all high in pectin, while strawberries, pears, elderberries, fresh apricots, and cherries have a low pectin content. Some fruits contain very little pectin, and so jams made using these fruits need additional help to set. Overripe fruit can also lower the pectin content and is not suitable for jams. It is, however, suitable for nectars, so use any fruit that is too ripe for jam to make a delicious nectar, cordial, or syrup.

The pectin content can be raised in various ways. Mixed-fruit jams can use the higher pectin content of one fruit to offset the lower content of another; lemon juice can be added at a rate of the juice of 1–2 lemons to every 4 pounds (1.8kg) of fruit, or bottled pectin can be used.

Preserving equipment

The principle underlying all preserving is to prevent decay caused by the growth of yeasts, molds, and bacteria. These organisms are destroyed when heated to sufficiently high temperatures to sterilize them, and, once sterilized, preserves must be kept securely sealed so that air cannot enter. Preserves that contain 60 percent or more of sugar are less susceptible to the growth of yeasts, which is why jams containing less sugar need to be eaten more quickly.

The jars
Once people discover you have become a jam maker, you will find yourself the happy recipient of empty jam jars of all shapes and sizes. The jars normally used for preserving in the United States are called mason jars. They have a screw-on lid consisting of two or more sections to help ensure a tight seal. These generally make the best containers for jams and jellies, while the European-style kilner jars are perfect for potting up chutneys and pickles. These have glass tops and a rubber seal that is secured by a thick wire clamp.

You can also use recycled jam or other condiment jars. Make sure, however, that the jars have no chips or cracks and that the lids fit securely. Corrosive materials must not come into contact with the preserve, especially if it contains vinegar (as used in chutneys and pickles), so make sure that the lids will not corrode.

The jars must be sterilized before use and a simple method is as follows. Wash the jars in hot soapy water, rinse in hot water, and leave to air-dry. Place a folded dish towel on an oven shelf and lay the jars on their sides on top. Shortly before you need to use them, heat the oven to 225°F (110°C), and leave the jars at this temperature for 30 minutes. The jars should still be hot when you fill them with hot jam.

Always prepare a few more jars than you think you will need, including some smaller jars to hold the last few spoonfuls of delicious preserve from the pan.

Other special equipment
There are a few items you can buy that will help for preserving:

Preserving pan
A noncorrosive, nonreactive preserving pan, big enough to hold large quantities of boiling jam, is a great investment. This type

of pan is wide and shallow to encourage rapid evaporation when bringing jam to setting point (see above). A good-quality pan will have a thick, heavy base, which will prevent any preserve from burning. While copper and aluminum pans are both popular, stainless steel is often regarded as the best, and it is certainly necessary when making preserves that contain vinegar.

When jam is brought to a rolling boil, it rises up in the pan, so never overfill the pan. If the pan is too small and overfilled, you will either end up with an overflowing mess of boiling syrupy jam or, in order to prevent this happening, you won't be able to raise the temperature high enough to reach setting point.

Double boiler
This item is particularly useful when making fruit curds and fruit syrups, nectars, and cordials. This can, however, be substituted for a simple heatproof bowl set over a pan of simmering water.

Jar funnel
This is essential for pouring hot jam safely into jars. Choose one small enough to fit into most of your jars but wide enough not to become clogged with pieces of fruit (see above). Sterilize and warm the funnel in the oven using the same method described on page 7 for preparing the jars. A sterilized, warmed scoop is also useful for ladling hot jam into the funnel.

Food mill
A good-quality food mill with several disks of various degrees of coarseness can be used to sieve fruit to extract the purée, which is excellent for making jams and gives a pleasing texture. They make puréeing apples a cinch, as you do not have to peel and core them first.

Jar lifter
Always use some form of projection when the jam is still hot. Special tongs, called a jar lifter, are used for handling the hot jars.

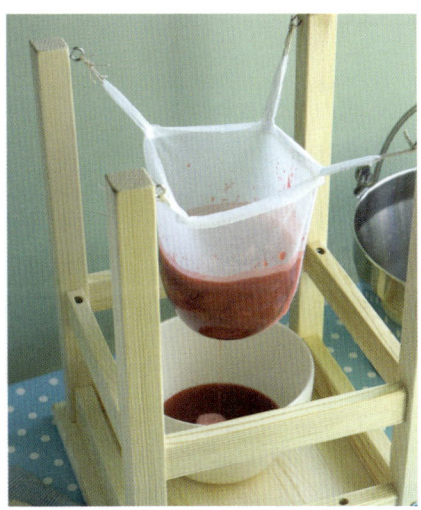 

Jelly bag
Ready-made jelly bags in a plastic stand that will fit over a bowl are ideal for straining the juices from cooked fruit, but you could also make your own version using muslin, nylon, a clean tea towel, or unbleached muslin tied across the legs of an upturned stool (see above).

Jam thermometer
Although not essential, this is useful for testing for setting point. Choose one that goes up to at least 230°F (110°C) and has a clip to attach it to the side of the pan.

Muslin
You will need squares of muslin to hold stones and spices that require cooking in with jams and chutneys. A generous square of fabric can be gathered together around the ingredients and tied into a bag with natural string or twine. Alternatively, you can buy little drawstring muslin bags made specifically for this purpose.

Sealing
Once poured into jars, hot jam should be sealed in some way. With screw-top jars, the seal forms part of the lid, but jars with ordinary lids require extra treatment. In Britain, waxed disks are used, which come in various sizes. In the United States, a layer of paraffin wax is preferred; this is readily available in stores where canning supplies are sold. Be sure to follow the manufacturer's instructions for melting and pouring the paraffin.

Labels
Label all your preserves so you know how long they have been stored. Chutneys and pickles, which benefit from a maturing period, also need to be labeled with this information. The stick-on labels and gift tags supplied at the back of this book are perfect to use on your first batch and they also act as pretty decoration if you are making condiments to give as gifts to friends and family.

PRESERVING EQUIPMENT

Preserving techniques

There are two basic methods for making jam. The traditional method involves cooking the fruit before adding the sugar and boiling to setting point. The macerating method requires leaving the fruit and sugar, which have a lower sugar-to-fruit ratio, together, ideally overnight, to draw out the juices and intensify the flavors, before boiling to a set. This method gives a softer-setting jam with a more syrupy consistency.

Jam: the traditional method

Cooking the fruit
Place the fruit in a preserving pan with some water, the quantity of which will vary with the type of fruit. Bush fruits may not need any water, as they quickly break up and release juices when heated and mashed with a spoon. Harder fruits need some water and a longer cooking time to soften them and release the pectin and acid. Simmer the fruits gently. Blueberries and plums should be cooked until their skins are soft. Once sugar is added, skins may become tough if they haven't been cooked enough before.

Adding the sugar
Use white granulated sugar. The amount of sugar needed varies, but the minimum amount recommended for 1 pound (450g) of bulky fruit (or about 3½ cups [450g] of bush fruits) is 1⅓ cups (270g). Ideally, use 1½–1¾ cups (400–475g) for a softer-set jam and 2 cups (550g) for a traditionally prepared jam. With experience you'll discover the effect you prefer.

To help the sugar dissolve quicker, warm it in a bowl in the oven (about 20 minutes on its lowest setting) before adding it to the fruit. Take the jam off the heat and allow it to cool slightly so it isn't still boiling when the sugar is added. Stir continuously over a low heat until the sugar has completely dissolved. (If the jam comes to the boil before the sugar has fully dissolved, it may crystalize during storage.)

Boiling the jam
When the sugar has dissolved, turn up the heat and bring the jam to the boil. The time this takes will vary, and is something that becomes more apparent with experience. Jam needs to maintain a high temperature to reduce and thicken so it will set as it cools. Sometimes this takes a matter of minutes, other times up to half an hour, depending on the amount of water in the jam. This stage is often referred to as a rolling boil.

Testing for setting point

After 5–10 minutes of rapid boiling, test the jam to see if it has reached setting point. This can be done in several ways (see below). Remove the pan from the heat while testing, so the jam doesn't overcook.

The cold plate test Put a small plate in the freezer to chill beforehand. Drip a pool of jam onto the plate with a spoon and allow it to cool for a few seconds (see right), then draw your finger through the jam. If setting point has been reached, the surface will wrinkle. When you raise your finger from the plate, the jam should form a strand, rather than dripping off.

Using a jam thermometer Dip the thermometer into hot water, then push it into the jam, preferably in the center of the pan. If the temperature reaches 220°F (105°C), setting point has been reached.

The flake test Dip a wooden spoon into the jam, then hold it above the pan. Leave it to cool for a few seconds, then let the jam fall off the spoon back into the pan. If the jam has a sticky consistency and forms strands or flakes that hang onto the spoon, setting point has been reached.

If setting point has not been reached, place the pan back on the heat and continue to boil rapidly, testing again at regular 5-minute intervals.

Skimming

During boiling, a scum sometimes forms on jam, jelly, or marmalade due to bubbles rising to the surface. This scum is harmless but can often spoil the appearance of the preserve. Stir in a small knob of butter to help disperse the scum or use a metal spoon to scoop it away.

Dispersing the fruit

Whole fruits or large pieces of fruit often rise up to the top of a jam, and as the jam sets, they are likely to stay put. If you are making a softer-set jam with pieces in, you may have to live with this, but for a thicker set, leave the jam for 5–10 minutes prior to placing in jars, then stir to distribute the pieces evenly.

Filling and storing

Have your hot jars and jar funnel ready. Pour the jam into the jars, leaving ¼ inch (5mm) between the top of the jam and the rim, if using a screw-top mason jar, or ½ inch (1cm) if sealing with waxed disks, paraffin wax, and ordinary lids (see page 9). Apply paraffin, if using, right away. If using mason jars or other canning jars, follow manufacturer's instructions for covering and sealing. Store the jam, once cool, in a dry, cool cabinet or pantry.

Jam: the macerating method

Allowing fruit and sugar to macerate together before cooking draws the moisture and juices from the fruit and preserves the flavor. Cooking times are reduced and flavors intensified, and it is possible to use a lower sugar content (see page 6), depending on the sweetness of the fruit.

Prepare the fruit as directed and place in a ceramic, glass, or stainless steel bowl. Add the sugar, cover with a plate, or push a piece of waxed or greaseproof paper down onto the surface of the fruit to hold in the moisture, and leave to macerate: softer fruits for 6–8 hours and harder fruits for up to 36 hours. You will see the sugar soak up the juices and a considerable amount of liquid begin to dissolve the sugar.

Pour the fruit into a preserving pan and stir over a gentle heat until the sugar has completely dissolved. Occasionally, the mixture is left to macerate again, but if not, bring the jam to setting point as for the traditional method and pour into the jars.

Making marmalade

If making citrus marmalade, it is important to cook the citrus rind properly, this can take 1½–3 hours, depending on the method you choose. Poaching the oranges whole is my preferred method, but removing the rind and shredding it at the outset is an alternative. If you use waxed fruits, you will need to scrub them well before use, but just a rinse will do for unwaxed ones.

Poaching

Wash the whole fruits and place in a heavy, lidded casserole dish with a tight-fitting lid. Pour in enough water to just cover the fruits, so they begin to float, then cover and place

in a preheated oven, 350°F (180°C), to poach for 2½–3 hours, by which time the skins will be softened. Leave until cool enough to handle, then, using a slotted spoon, lift the fruits from the liquid, halve them, and scoop out the insides, gathering together all the pith and seeds and collecting any juice. Slice the rind into strips. Place the seeds and pith in a square of muslin, and tie into a bundle with string. Pour any collected juice back in with the cooking liquid.

Paring the rind first

Cut the uncooked fruits in half and squeeze out and collect the juice. Save the seeds. Pare the rind and chop into thin shreds. Chop the pith finely. Place the seeds in a square of muslin and tie into a bundle with string. Place everything in a pan and add enough water to cover, then leave overnight to soak. The next day, bring to the boil, then simmer for about 1½ hours until the rind is softened and cooked through. Remove the bundle of seeds. From now on, the method is the same whichever form of preparation you used. Add warmed sugar and stir to dissolve, then complete in the same way as if making jam. Once setting point is reached, leave the marmalade for 10–15 minutes, then remove the muslin bag (if using the poaching method) and stir to distribute the rind shreds before pouring into jars.

Making jellies

A jelly is similar to a jam but without pieces of fruit. The fruit is cooked with water, then poured into a jelly bag and allowed to drip through. Only the juice is used. Fruits most suited to jelly making generally have a high pectin content (see page 6).

When making jellies, cook the fruit first with water until tender. You can mash the fruit with a spoon at this stage before pouring it into a jelly bag suspended over a container to catch the drips. For the clearest jelly, allow plenty of time for the juice to drip through (overnight is ideal), and don't squeeze the bag, as this will make the jelly cloudy. (It is often possible to reboil the contents of the jelly bag using half the original amount of water and pour it through the bag again to get the maximum amount of juice and pectin from the fruit.)

Now measure the juice to work out how much sugar will be needed. The general rule is ¾ cup (200g) sugar to every 1 cup (250ml) juice, which makes roughly 1⅝ pounds (750g) jelly. Place the juice in a preserving pan and add warmed sugar as for jam-making, stirring until completely dissolved. Bring to a rapid boil and cook on a high heat to reach settting point, as before. Rather than waste the residue in the jelly bag, push it through a food mill, collect the purée, sweeten it, and use for pie fillings.

Making curds

Fruit curds have shorter keeping times than jams and jellies—2 months unopened in a cool place. Make them in small jars, for once opened, they should be kept in the refrigerator and eaten within 2 weeks. You can also pour curds into suitable containers and freeze them for 6 months.

Curds are made using sugar, butter, and eggs, so are more like a custard than a jam. They are best suited to tart, fruity flavors. So that the eggs don't curdle or cook on too high a heat, it is best to use a double boiler or a basin set over a pan of simmering water. You will have to stir the curd continuously for 20–30 minutes until it thickens and will coat the back of the spoon, but the result will be well worth the effort.

Prepare a fruit purée first by cooking the fruit in the minimum amount of water, if any at all, until tender. Softer fruits, such as raspberries and blueberries, require little cooking, while squash need more. Press the fruit through the fine disk of a food mill or a sieve and collect the purée.

Making chutneys and pickles

Chutneys are made from fruits and vegetables mixed with vinegar, sugar, and spices. They are easy to make, generally just requiring all the ingredients to be thrown together in a preserving pan and cooked for a couple of hours. It is important to pack them in jars with vinegar-proof lids.

Try to leave chutneys and pickles to mature for 6–8 weeks, or even a few months, before eating, as the flavors mellow over time.

Pickles and chutneys both require vinegars flavored with spices, and the recipes in this book give instructions for making these from scratch. However, you can also make your own vinegars using the recipes that follow—two for pickling vinegars and two for sweetened pickling vinegars, which are ideal for pickling fruits and fruit chutneys.

Pickling vinegar

To 1 quart (1 liter) cider, malt, or wine vinegar, add:
piece of fresh gingeroot approx. ¾ x 2½ inches (20g), peeled and finely sliced
1 tbsp each black peppercorns, mustard seeds, celery seeds
8 dried red chilies
2 tsp each whole allspice, whole cloves, whole coriander seeds

Mix all the spices together and divide between clean, sterilized bottles. Fill the bottles with the vinegar and seal with corks or stoppers. Leave the vinegar to infuse for 6–8 weeks, giving the bottles an occasional shake. Strain out the spices from the vinegar before using.

For a quicker version Put all the ingredients in a bowl and place this over a pan of simmering water, or use a double boiler. Allow the vinegar to warm through without boiling, then remove it from the heat and leave the spices to steep in the warm vinegar for 2–3 hours. Strain out the spices from the vinegar before using.

Sweet pickling vinegar

To 1 quart (1 liter) cider, malt, or wine vinegar, add:
1 cinnamon stick
1 tbsp each whole allspice, whole coriander seeds, whole cloves, white peppercorns
5 blades of mace
2 dried red chilies (optional)
3½ cups (800g) brown or white sugar

Mix the spices together and divide between clean bottles. Warm the vinegar and dissolve the sugar in it, then fill the bottles with the vinegar and seal with corks or stoppers. Leave to infuse for 6–8 weeks, giving the bottles an occasional shake. Strain out the spices from the vinegar before using.

For a quicker version Place 2½ cups (600ml) white wine vinegar, a rounded ¾ cup (200g) of sugar, a ¾-inch (1cm) square piece of fresh gingerroot, and a few whole allspice berries and black peppercorns in a pan, then stir over a low heat to dissolve the sugar. Turn up the heat and boil for 1 minute, then remove from the heat. Strain the spices from the vinegar before using.

Making nectars and cordials

Nectars and cordials make good use of fruit that is overripe and therefore not suitable for jam-making; they are also very easy to make. Bush fruits, such as blackberries, loganberries, and raspberries, are perfectly suitred for making nectars, as are citrus fruits and foraged ingredients, such as rose hips, elderflowers, and elderberries.

For all bush fruits the method is the same. Put the fruit in a bowl and break it up with a spoon, then add only a minimal amount of water, if any at all. Place the bowl over a pan of simmering water and heat through to extract all the juice from the fruit. Pour the fruit through a jelly bag and collect the juice underneath, leaving it to drip overnight.

Add a scant 1½ cups (350g) sugar to every 2 cups (500ml) juice and stir together over a low heat until dissolved; do not allow it to boil. Strain into clean bottles, filling to within 1 inch (2.5cm) of the top of the bottle. Cork securely or use bottles with ceramic stoppers and wires. The bottles will now need to be sterilized so that the contents keep for a long time. (Alternatively—and this is the more straightforward option—the cordial or nectar can be poured into suitable containers and frozen.)

To sterilize, place some folded newspaper or a trivet in the bottom of a pan and place the bottles on top. Add cold water almost to the top of the bottles, then bring to the boil and simmer for 20 minutes. Make sure that the bottles are securely sealed, then store them in a cool, dry place.

Keeping times

The jams and jellies will keep, unopened, in a cool, dark place for at least 6 months, and the other preserves will keep for around 6–12 months. Keeping times will vary once jars and bottles are opened, but you will find that because these preserves are so delicious they will undoubtedly be eaten up long before there is any chance of their deteriorating.

PRESERVING TECHNIQUES

Problem solving

Why jam goes moldy
Mold is most often caused by a failure to seal the jam adequately while it is still very hot. Alternatively, jars may have been damp or cold when used, weren't filled right to the top, or have been stored in a damp place. Other possible causes are insufficient evaporation of water during the preliminary cooking and/or too short a period of boiling after the sugar has been added. Jam with a good set is less likely to go moldy, while a softer-set jam will be more inclined to spoil. Sometimes mold can form because the fruit was picked on a wet day. Mold is not harmful to the jam but it may affect the taste slightly. If it is removed, the jam can be boiled up again and re-packed in clean, sterilized jars.

Why fruit rises in the jam
When the fruit is in big pieces or is used whole, such as strawberries and cherries, the pieces tend to rise in the jam after it is poured. To keep them dispersed throughout the preserve, leave the jam in the pan for 10–15 minutes after setting point is reached to thicken slightly, then stir to redistribute before pouring it into the jars. The syrupy consistency of softer-set jams means that fruit will invariably rise to the top of the jar. The same problem may occur with the rind in marmalade, and the solution of waiting and stirring is exactly the same.

Why tiny bubbles appear
Bubbles indicate fermentation, which is usually the result of too little sugar in relation to the quantity of fruit. When jam is not reduced sufficiently, this can also affect the proportion of sugar.

Why jam crystallizes
Too much sugar or too little acid is usually the cause. Low-acid fruits benefit from the addition of acid in the form of lemon juice. Making sure that the sugar has dissolved completely before bringing the jam to a fast boil also helps. Sometimes overripe fruit is responsible, or storing the jam in too warm a place.

Why jam won't set
Low levels of pectin, due to using fruits containing very little pectin or overripe fruit, may make it difficult to reach setting point. Other reasons include under-boiling the fruit, so that the pectin is not fully extracted, or insufficient evaporation of the water before the sugar is added, in which case return the jam to the preserving pan and boil it further. It is also possible to overcook jam after sugar has been added, for which there is no remedy. For fruits low in pectin, such as strawberries and cherries, you can increase the pectin content in the form of other fruits (such as lemon juice, apples, or redcurrants).

Why jam shrinks in the jar
Shrinkage is caused by the jam being inadequately covered or sealed, or failure to store it in a cool, dark, and dry place.

1. Jams & jellies

Jam is simply a term used to describe fruit and sugar cooked together so it will keep, while jellies are made from the juices extracted from the fruit and have a clarity and purity that is very attractive. Making your own jams and jellies is a great way to use up some of the excess fruit you grow yourself or ask friends to share with you some of their home-grown produce.

Jams and jellies are really versatile, and are at home with both sweet and savory food. Nothing beats high tea on a summer afternoon, with a scone or biscuit covered in a dollop of homemade strawberry jam in one hand and a cup of tea in the other. Or try experimenting with more unusual ingredients like rowan berries and serve them with game. Delicious!

Strawberry & vanilla jam

Let's face it, strawberry jam is the real classic. This fragile fruit isn't a great keeper, so for the best jam capture the fruit at its freshest, preserving it in recognizable chunks. This really is summer in a jar. Here I have teamed strawberries with vanilla, the perfect partner, which as far as I'm concerned you can't ever get enough of.

This recipe uses slightly less sugar than a traditional strawberry jam might and consequently has a softer set, which means if you are feeling really gluttonous, you can eat it straight from the jar. Or swirl a few spoonfuls through a mixture of mascarpone and plain yogurt for a fast dessert. Or dollop it onto a freshly baked biscuit or scone—eating it quickly before the jam oozes away over the sides.

Makes about 4 cups (1.3kg)

1 vanilla bean (pod)

4 pints (1kg) strawberries, hulled; larger fruits halved

3 scant cups (750g) sugar

juice of 3 small lemons

1 Split the vanilla bean lengthwise into four pieces and place in a bowl with the strawberries, tucking the bean pieces in among the fruit. Cover with the sugar and leave for 12 hours or overnight.

2 Pour the fruit, vanilla bean, and juice into a preserving pan and add the lemon juice. Cook over a low heat until the sugar has dissolved, stirring only now and then so that the fruit stays intact. Turn up the heat and boil rapidly to reach setting point (see page 11). Skim if necessary (see page 11).

3 Remove the vanilla bean pieces, scrape the seeds out of them, and add these to the jam, disposing of the beans. Stir the seeds through the jam.

4 Pour the jam into hot, sterilized jars (see page 7) and seal (see page 11).

Cherry jam

You can use a black cooking cherry, such as a Morello cherry, for this jam, or a paler dessert cherry, and the color of your jam will vary accordingly. If you grow your own, make sure to pick them as soon as they ripen, or the birds will eat all of them before you get the chance.

Makes about 3 cups (900g)

2 pints (700g) cherries

1 generous cup (500g) warmed sugar (see page 10)

1 tbsp lemon juice

1 Pit the cherries, using a cherry stoner over a basin to catch any juice. Place the stones in a piece of muslin and tie it into a bag with string. Put the fruit and juice into a pan with 2 tablespoons water and simmer gently until the fruit is just cooked.

2 Add the warmed sugar and the lemon juice to the fruit and stir over a low heat until all the sugar has dissolved, then turn up the heat and boil rapidly to reach setting point (see page 11). Remove the muslin bag and leave the jam for 5–10 minutes, then stir to redistribute the cherries. Skim if necessary (see page 11).

3 Pour the jam into hot, sterilized jars (see page 7) and seal (see page 11).

Blackberry jelly

Children seem to love collecting blackberries, so put them to work gathering the fruit for this jelly. Often blackberry jelly has added spices, but I always prefer the real fruit taste to dominate, so here I have opted for the pure fruit, with just a hint of lemon to help it set.

For quantity, see page 13

5 pints (1.4kg) blackberries

juice of ½ lemon

sugar (for quantity see step 3)

1 Place the berries in a preserving pan with scant ½ cup (100ml) water. Simmer the fruit for 5 minutes until soft, mashing the berries with a wooden spoon.

2 Pour the fruit into a jelly bag, suspended over a measuring pitcher to catch the drips, and leave for several hours or overnight until the pulp left in the bag is almost dry.

3 Allow ¾ (450g) cup sugar for every 1 cup of juice. Add the lemon juice to the blackberry juice and pour into a preserving pan. Add the sugar and stir over a gentle heat until it is completely dissolved, then turn up the heat and boil rapidly to reach setting point (see page 11).

4 Skim if necessary (see page 11). Pour the jelly into hot, sterilized jars (see page 7) and seal (see page 11).

Raspberry jelly

This jelly is the most wondrous, jewel-like color and is superbly fruity, which makes it ideal for using as the filling in a layer cake. It also suits anyone who likes raspberries but hates their seeds.

Follow the instructions for Blackberry Jelly above, substituting raspberries for the blackberries

White currant & red chili jam

White currants are another fruit with a lovely tart flavor, which makes them just perfect for jam making. This jam, with its additional chili kick, is subtle enough to eat on sourdough toast for breakfast but could also be taken up a notch, by adding more chili to taste, and serving as a relish to go with cheese. And if you have a few red gooseberries to add to the currants, they'll give this jam a beautiful rose hue.

Makes about 3½ cups (1.3kg)

3 pints (1kg) white currants

4 red gooseberries (optional)

juice of 1 lemon

2 red chilies (or more if you wish), deseeded and finely chopped

warmed sugar (see page 10; for quantity see step 3)

1 Strip the white currants from their stalks by running the tines of a fork over their stems. Place the currants and gooseberries, if using, in a pan along with the lemon juice and ⅝ cup (150ml) water. Simmer until the fruits are soft and bursting.

2 Push the fruit through the fine disk of a food mill, or a sieve, collecting the resulting purée in a measuring pitcher or jug.

3 Allow ¾ (450g) cup sugar to every 1 cup (600ml) purée.

4 Gently heat the purée and add the chopped chilies, then the warmed sugar. Stir the jam over a low heat until the sugar has completely dissolved. Turn up the heat and boil rapidly to reach setting point (see page 11). Skim if necessary (see page 11).

5 Pour the jam into hot, sterilized jars (see page 7) and seal (see page 11).

Recipe name

Ingredients

Recipe

Quantity made

Comments

Recipe name

Ingredients

Recipe

Quantity made

Comments

JAMS & JELLIES

Recipe name

Ingredients

Recipe

Quantity made

Comments

Recipe name

Ingredients

Recipe

Quantity made

Comments

Recipe name

Ingredients

Recipe

Quantity made

Comments

Recipe name

Ingredients

Recipe

Quantity made

Comments

JAMS & JELLIES

Recipe name

Ingredients

Recipe

Quantity made

Comments

Recipe name

Ingredients

Recipe

Quantity made

Comments

Recipe name

Ingredients

Recipe

Quantity made

Comments

Recipe name

Ingredients

Recipe

Quantity made

Comments

Recipe name

Ingredients

Recipe

Quantity made

Comments

Recipe name

Ingredients

Recipe

Quantity made

Comments

Recipe name

Ingredients

Recipe

Quantity made

Comments

Recipe name

Ingredients

Recipe

Quantity made

Comments

JAMS & JELLIES

Recipe name

Ingredients

Recipe

Quantity made

Comments

Recipe name

Ingredients

Recipe

Quantity made

Comments

Recipe name

Ingredients

Recipe

Quantity made

Comments

Recipe name

Ingredients

Recipe

Quantity made

Comments

Recipe name

Ingredients

Recipe name

Ingredients

Recipe

Recipe

Quantity made

Comments

Quantity made

Comments

Recipe name

Ingredients

Recipe

Quantity made

Comments

Recipe name

Ingredients

Recipe

Quantity made

Comments

Recipe name

Ingredients

Recipe

Quantity made

Comments

Recipe name

Ingredients

Recipe

Quantity made

Comments

Recipe name

Ingredients

Recipe

Quantity made

Comments

Recipe name

Ingredients

Recipe

Quantity made

Comments

JAMS & JELLIES

Recipe name

Ingredients

Recipe

Quantity made

Comments

Recipe name

Ingredients

Recipe

Quantity made

Comments

Recipe name

Ingredients

Recipe name

Ingredients

Recipe

Recipe

Quantity made

Comments

Quantity made

Comments

JAMS & JELLIES

JAMS & JELLIES

Recipe name

Ingredients

Recipe

Quantity made

Comments

Recipe name

Ingredients

Recipe

Quantity made

Comments

Recipe name

Ingredients

Recipe

Quantity made

Comments

Recipe name

Ingredients

Recipe

Quantity made

Comments

JAMS & JELLIES

Recipe name

Ingredients

Recipe

Quantity made

Comments

Recipe name

Ingredients

Recipe

Quantity made

Comments

Recipe name

Ingredients

Recipe name

Ingredients

Recipe

Recipe

Quantity made

Comments

Quantity made

Comments

JAMS & JELLIES

Recipe name

Ingredients

Recipe

Quantity made

Comments

Recipe name

Ingredients

Recipe

Quantity made

Comments

2. Curds & marmalades

Curds and marmalades are great any time of day, whether served as a dessert in teaspoon-sized portions in bite-sized sweet pastry cases or spread over your toast for breakfast in the morning. Curds are little pots of fruity loveliness that are totally delicious and are guaranteed not to hang around for long after they've been made.

Marmalades usually refer to a preserve made from citrus fruits, with orange being the classic, but other varieties, such as onion marmalade, are becoming increasingly popular and taste great with cheese or melted over sausages. The first marmalade was made from quinces and had Portuguese origins, while in France marmalade tends to be made from other puréed fruits.

Lemon curd

An outstanding classic, this sharp lemon curd makes the perfect filling for an open tart. It can also be spread between the layers of a cake, or swirled through vanilla ice cream. Utter perfection, whichever way you serve it.

Makes about 1¼ cups (400g)

zest and juice of 3 lemons

6 tbsp (85g) butter, preferably unsalted, cut into cubes

⅞ cup (200g) fine granulated sugar

3 large eggs, beaten

1 Place the lemon zest and juice in a bowl set over a pan of simmering water (or use a double boiler) along with the butter and sugar. Add the beaten eggs, pouring them through a sieve.

2 Stir with a wooden spoon until everything becomes heated through and well blended. Continue cooking, stirring constantly, until the curd thickens enough to coat the back of the spoon—this should take about 15–20 minutes.

3 Pour the curd into small, hot, sterilized jars (see page 7) and seal (see page 11).

Bitter orange curd

The bitter nature of Seville oranges works perfectly for a curd. Most sweet oranges just don't have enough character to use in this way, although blood oranges have more of a flavor kick than other sweet varieties, so they work well also. Use the curd as a filling for a sweet pastry tart, or spread it liberally between the layers or a rich chocolate cake, or simply serve it on a thick slice of fresh bread.

Makes about 1 cup (350g)

zest and juice of 3 Seville oranges

3 tbsp (slightly rounded) (50g) butter, preferably unsalted, cut into chunks

¾ cup (170g) fine granulated sugar

2 large eggs, beaten

Follow the instructions above for making Lemon Curd using the ingredients to the left.

Seville orange marmalade

Seville oranges are available for a short time only, in late winter, but they do make the best marmalade, which makes finding them worth the effort. Because of their extremely bitter taste, they are used only for cooking, but it is this robust quality that makes them particularly good when cooked and sweetened.

Makes about 6 cups (2kg)

2 pounds (1kg) Seville oranges

1 small lemon

6 cups (1.5kg) sugar

1 Preheat the oven to 350°F (180°C). Place the whole fruits in a heavy, lidded casserole or a preserving pan that will fit in the oven. Pour in 5 cups (1.25 liters) of water and bring to simmering point.

2 Cover the pan (if using a preserving pan, make a lid from aluminum foil), and place in the oven. Poach the fruit for 2½–3 hours, by which time the skins will be soft.

3 Using a spoon, lift the fruit out of the liquid into a colander. When cool enough to handle, cut each fruit in half and scoop out the pulp with a spoon, leaving just the peel, placing the pulp, pith, and seeds in a muslin bag suspended over a bowl to catch any drips. (Alternatively, use a large piece of muslin gathered into a bag and tied with string). Measure the liquid, adding any collected in the bowl under the drained pulp, and if necessary add water to make it up to 1 quart (1 liter).

4 Place the muslin bag in a saucepan with enough poaching liquid to cover. Bring to the boil and simmer for 15 minutes. Leave until cool enough to handle, then squeeze the bag to get as much of the liquid as possible from the pulp. Discard the bag and its contents.

5 Chop the rind into thin strips and put into a preserving pan. Add all the poaching liquid. If the mixture is cold, you can add the sugar without warming it; otherwise you will need to warm the sugar first (see page 10). Stir the sugar into the orange liquid over a low heat until it is completely dissolved and the liquid is clear, then boil rapidly for 15 minutes and test for setting point (see page 11).

6 Turn off the heat and leave to stand for 15 minutes, then stir to distribute the peel. Skim if necessary (see page 11). Pour into hot, sterilized jars (see page 7) and seal (see page 11).

Peach marmalade

I usually choose a tangy citrus preserve to spread on my toast at breakfast, but this aromatic, slightly gentler marmalade makes a lovely start to the day. You can, of course, eat it any time, but it has become one of my morning favorites. The cooking brings out the superb aroma of the fruit; and the variation below, including vanilla, produces an even more sybaritic experience.

Makes about 4 cups (1.3kg)

2 pounds (900g) peaches, roughly chopped

3¼ cups (750g) sugar

1 Place the peaches and their stones in a pan along with 1 cup (250ml) water. Bring them to simmering point and simmer until the peach pieces are soft.

2 Discard the stones and press the flesh through the fine disk of a food mill, or a sieve, to give a purée.

3 Put the purée into a preserving pan, add the sugar, warmed if necessary (see page 50, step 5), and stir gently over a low heat until the sugar has completely dissolved. Turn up the heat and boil until it reaches setting point (see page 11). Skim mixture if necessary (see page 11).

4 Pour the marmalade into hot, sterilized jars (see page 7) and seal (see page 11).

Butternut & ginger curd

Squashes and pumpkins are naturally sweet, so ideal for making into sweet preserves. Here butternut squash is the main ingredient, but other types can be used instead. The brighter orange the flesh, the better. Chopped pieces of stem ginger add a lovely bite to the texture.

Makes about 1½ cups (1.4kg)

1 small butternut squash, peeled, deseeded, and roughly chopped

zest and juice of 1 lemon

zest and juice of 1 orange

4 tbsp plus 1 tsp (70g) butter, preferably unsalted, cut into cubes

⅞ cup (200g) fine granulated sugar

2 large eggs plus 2 yolks, beaten

4 pieces of stem ginger, approx. 1 inch in diameter (75g), finely chopped

3 tbsp syrup from the stem ginger

1 Place the squash in a pan with ½ cup (100ml) water to stop it from sticking to the pan as it cooks. Cover and cook until soft, then pour off any excess liquid.

2 Purée the squash in a food processor or pass it through the fine disk of a food mill. Alternatively, press it through a sieve.

3 Measure out 1¼ cups (300g) of the squash purée and place this in a bowl over simmering water (or use a double boiler), along with all the other ingredients, pouring the beaten eggs through a sieve onto the purée. Continue stirring with a wooden spoon until everything becomes well blended, the sugar is dissolved, and the curd thickens and will coat the back of the spoon—this should take about 30 minutes.

4 Pour the curd into small, hot, sterilized jars (see page 7) and seal (see page 11).

Recipe name

Ingredients

Recipe name

Ingredients

Recipe

Quantity made

Comments

Recipe

Quantity made

Comments

CURDS & MARMALADES

CURDS & MARMALADES

Recipe name

Ingredients

Recipe

Quantity made

Comments

Recipe name

Ingredients

Recipe

Quantity made

Comments

Recipe name

Ingredients

Recipe

Quantity made
Comments

Recipe name

Ingredients

Recipe

Quantity made
Comments

CURDS & MARMALADES

CURDS & MARMALADES

Recipe name

Ingredients

Recipe

Quantity made

Comments

Recipe name

Ingredients

Recipe

Quantity made

Comments

Recipe name

Ingredients

Recipe

Quantity made

Comments

Recipe name

Ingredients

Recipe

Quantity made

Comments

CURDS & MARMALADES

CURDS & MARMALADES

Recipe name

Ingredients

Recipe

Quantity made

Comments

Recipe name

Ingredients

Recipe

Quantity made

Comments

Recipe name

Ingredients

Recipe

Quantity made

Comments

Recipe name

Ingredients

Recipe

Quantity made

Comments

CURDS & MARMALADES

Recipe name

Ingredients

Recipe

Quantity made

Comments

Recipe name

Ingredients

Recipe

Quantity made

Comments

Recipe name

Ingredients

Recipe

Quantity made

Comments

Recipe name

Ingredients

Recipe

Quantity made

Comments

CURDS & MARMALADES

Recipe name

Ingredients

Recipe

Quantity made

Comments

Recipe name

Ingredients

Recipe

Quantity made

Comments

Recipe name

Ingredients

Recipe

Quantity made

Comments

Recipe name

Ingredients

Recipe

Quantity made

Comments

CURDS & MARMALADES

Recipe name

Ingredients

Recipe

Quantity made

Comments

Recipe name

Ingredients

Recipe

Quantity made

Comments

Recipe name

Ingredients

Recipe

Quantity made

Comments

Recipe name

Ingredients

Recipe

Quantity made

Comments

CURDS & MARMALADES

CURDS & MARMALADES

Recipe name

Ingredients

Recipe

Quantity made

Comments

Recipe name

Ingredients

Recipe

Quantity made

Comments

Recipe name

Ingredients

Recipe

Quantity made

Comments

Recipe name

Ingredients

Recipe

Quantity made

Comments

CURDS & MARMALADES

CURDS & MARMALADES

Recipe name

Ingredients

Recipe

Quantity made

Comments

Recipe name

Ingredients

Recipe

Quantity made

Comments

Recipe name

Ingredients

Recipe

Quantity made

Comments

Recipe name

Ingredients

Recipe

Quantity made

Comments

CURDS & MARMALADES

CURDS & MARMALADES

Recipe name

Ingredients

Recipe

Quantity made

Comments

Recipe name

Ingredients

Recipe

Quantity made

Comments

3. Chutneys & pickles

Chutneys and cheese are firm friends that always bring out the best in each other. They also are a great accompaniment to any plate of cold meat. Chutneys are simple because making them is not an exact science, you can adjust the spices and sweetness to suit your tastes. They require a long cooking time in order to reach a rich, thick consistency, but it will be worth the wait.

When it comes to pickles, vinegar is the star ingredient. Vinegar comes into its own here and the more matured and spiced it is, the better (see page 14 for recipe ideas). You can use any kind of vinegar but cider vinegar goes well with apples and pears, malt vinegar with darker pickles, and white wine vinegar helps the color of ingredients to be seen at their best.

Mango chutney

A classic accompaniment to Indian food, this sticky sweet chutney is unbeatable. This is a great way of using mangoes when slightly underripe, if, like me, you aren't ever quite sure whether your mangoes are ripe enough to eat.

Makes about 5¼ cups (1.7kg)

2 pounds (1.2kg) mango flesh, when peeled and stoned (about 4 pounds [1.8kg] unstoned)

2 tsp mixed pickling spices

juice and thickly pared rind of 1 small orange

½ pound (350g) onions, finely chopped

1¼ cups (300ml) white wine vinegar

2 cloves garlic

1 tbsp grated gingerroot

2 hot red chilies, deseeded and minced

2⅜ cups (550g) (packed) warmed good-quality light brown (muscavado) sugar (see page 10)

1 Cut half of the mango flesh into small pieces and leave the other half in larger chunks. Put the pickling spices and rind pieces in a piece of muslin and tie it into a bag.

2 Place all the ingredients except the sugar and large mango chunks in a stainless steel preserving pan and simmer gently for 20 minutes until the mango and onions are soft.

3 Add the rest of the mango and simmer gently for another 5 minutes. Add the warmed sugar and stir over a low heat until it has completely dissolved, then boil until the mixture reaches a thick, jamlike consistency, stirring gently and taking care to retain the chunky texture.

4 Remove the muslin bag. Allow the chutney to cool for 10 minutes, then stir again to redistribute the bits.

5 Pour the chutney into hot, sterilized jars (see page 7) and seal (see page 11).

Pumpkin chutney

With their wonderful shapes, textures, and vibrant colors, pumpkins and squashes are always so visually appealing and their flesh gives this chutney a colorful look and sweeter flavor, which is always a good thing.

Makes about 6½ cups (2kg)

12 peppercorns

2 tsp whole allspice

¾-inch- (2cm-) square piece of fresh gingerroot, bruised

5½ cups (750g) pumpkin flesh, cut into ⅝-inch (1-cm) cubes (from pumpkin weighing approx. 2¾ pounds [1.25kg])

1 pound (450g) cooking apples, peeled, cored, and finely chopped

2 rounded tbsp (50g) finely chopped stem ginger

¾ pound (350g) shallots, peeled, cored, and finely chopped

1⅜ cup (200g) golden raisins or sultanas, chopped

2 cloves garlic, finely chopped

2 tsp salt

2½ cups (600ml) cider vinegar

1⅞ cups (packed) (400g) warmed soft brown (muscavado) sugar (see page 10)

1 Place the dry spices and gingerroot in a piece of muslin and tie it into a bag with string. Place all the ingredients except the sugar in a stainless steel preserving pan and bring slowly to the boil, then simmer gently for 20 minutes until the pumpkin and apple are soft.

2 Add the warmed sugar and stir over a gentle heat until all the sugar has dissolved, then turn up the heat and simmer for approximately 1–1½ hours until the chutney is thick but still juicy, stirring occasionally.

3 Remove the muslin bag, then pour the chutney into hot, sterilized jars (see page 7) and seal (see page 11).

Pickled shallots

Pickled onions are a classic British pickle and one that seems to be popular with children and adults alike. They go with just about anything, but a simple lunch made up of a piece of crusty bread, a wedge of sharp cheese, and some pickled onions is a combination that is hard to beat. In order for your onions to retain that initial crunch, they need to be marinated in brine for a few days before being packed into jars and covered in spiced vinegar. Apart from that, this pickle has to be the easiest there is, and you should always keep a few jars on the pantry shelf.

Makes about 3 cups

2 pounds (1kg) shallots

½ (rounded) cup (250g) salt

2⅓ cups (600ml) pickling vinegar (see page 14)

1 Place the shallots in a large bowl without skinning them. Make the brine by dissolving half of the salt in 1 quart (2 pints) water, then pour this over the shallots and leave for 12 hours. Drain and skin the shallots.

2 Make a second batch of brine using the remaining salt and the same amount of water, pour it over the shallots, and leave for another 2–3 days.

3 Meanwhile, if you don't already have some pickling vinegar steeping in a cabinet, make a batch of the quick version a while before the brining period is due to finish; leave this until cold.

4 Drain and rinse the salt from the onions and pack them tightly into sterilized jars (see page 7). Pour the cold pickling vinegar over them so that they are completely covered. Cover and seal the jars (see page 11). The shallots will keep their flavor and crispness for up to 6 months after they have been bottled.

Green tomato & red onion chutney

At the end of the season, when there is no more heat left outside to ripen the last of the tomatoes, it is time to bring them into the house. If you place them on any empty windowsill you can find, there's a chance that the last precious fruits will slowly turn from green to red. Packing them in boxes, spaced apart in layers with straw or woolen material between them, is another way of ripening them gradually and prolonging the season; but if you have plenty to spare, the still-green ones are just perfect for turning into chutney.

Makes about 5¼ cups (1.75kg)

2 pounds (1kg) green tomatoes

½ pound (250g) cooking apples, peeled and cored

1 pound (450g) red onions, roughly chopped

¾ cup (200g) rounded (packed) soft brown sugar

2½ cups (600ml) malt vinegar

½ tsp mustard seeds

½ tsp cayenne pepper

1 tbsp finely grated fresh gingerroot

1¼ cups (200g) raisins

3 green chilies, deseeded and finely chopped

1 tsp salt

1 To skin the tomatoes, place them in a bowl and pour boiling water over them, then leave for a minute or two. The skins should now slide off the fruits when you cut into them with a sharp knife. It is harder to remove the skins from the tomatoes when they are green, so steeping them for longer than usual will help. Chop the tomatoes roughly.

2 Place all the ingredients in a stainless steel preserving pan and bring to the boil. Reduce the heat and simmer until everything is cooked and the chutney has thickened, stirring occasionally.

3 Pour the chutney into hot, sterilized jars (see page 7) and seal (see page 11).

Recipe name
Picallili

Ingredients
300g Cauli
300g Beans
300g Cagette
200g Peppers
250g Shallots

Recipe
Olive Magazine
online

doubled

Quantity made 12 jars
Comments
Made Jul 2020

Recipe name

Ingredients

Recipe

Quantity made
Comments

CHUTNEYS & PICKLES

Recipe name

Ingredients

Recipe

Quantity made

Comments

Recipe name

Ingredients

Recipe

Quantity made

Comments

Recipe name

Ingredients

Recipe

Quantity made

Comments

Recipe name

Ingredients

Recipe

Quantity made

Comments

CHUTNEYS & PICKLES

Recipe name

Ingredients

Recipe

Quantity made

Comments

Recipe name

Ingredients

Recipe

Quantity made

Comments

Recipe name

Ingredients

Recipe

Quantity made

Comments

Recipe name

Ingredients

Recipe

Quantity made

Comments

CHUTNEYS & PICKLES

Recipe name

Ingredients

Recipe

Quantity made

Comments

Recipe name

Ingredients

Recipe

Quantity made

Comments

Recipe name

Ingredients

Recipe

Quantity made

Comments

Recipe name

Ingredients

Recipe

Quantity made

Comments

CHUTNEYS & PICKLES

CHUTNEYS & PICKLES

Recipe name

Ingredients

Recipe

Quantity made

Comments

Recipe name

Ingredients

Recipe

Quantity made

Comments

Recipe name

Ingredients

Recipe

Quantity made
Comments

Recipe name

Ingredients

Recipe

Quantity made
Comments

CHUTNEYS & PICKLES

Recipe name

Ingredients

Recipe

Quantity made

Comments

Recipe name

Ingredients

Recipe

Quantity made

Comments

Recipe name

Ingredients

Recipe

Quantity made

Comments

Recipe name

Ingredients

Recipe

Quantity made

Comments

CHUTNEYS & PICKLES

Recipe name

Ingredients

Recipe

Quantity made

Comments

Recipe name

Ingredients

Recipe

Quantity made

Comments

Recipe name

Ingredients

Recipe

Quantity made

Comments

Recipe name

Ingredients

Recipe

Quantity made

Comments

CHUTNEYS & PICKLES

CHUTNEYS & PICKLES

Recipe name

Ingredients

Recipe

Quantity made

Comments

Recipe name

Ingredients

Recipe

Quantity made

Comments

Recipe name

Ingredients

Recipe

Quantity made

Comments

Recipe name

Ingredients

Recipe

Quantity made

Comments

CHUTNEYS & PICKLES

Recipe name

Ingredients

Recipe

Quantity made

Comments

Recipe name

Ingredients

Recipe

Quantity made

Comments

Recipe name

Ingredients

Recipe

Quantity made

Comments

Recipe name

Ingredients

Recipe

Quantity made

Comments

CHUTNEYS & PICKLES

Recipe name

Ingredients

Recipe

Quantity made

Comments

Recipe name

Ingredients

Recipe

Quantity made

Comments

Recipe name

Ingredients

Recipe

Quantity made

Comments

Recipe name

Ingredients

Recipe

Quantity made

Comments

CHUTNEYS & PICKLES

Recipe name

Ingredients

Recipe

Quantity made

Comments

Recipe name

Ingredients

Recipe

Quantity made

Comments

4. Nectars & cordials

Nectars, cordials, and syrups are, in fact, the same thing. These sweetened fruity concentrates are delicious diluted with water, added to milk for milk shakes, poured over ice cream, or swirled through cake mixture prior to baking for a marbled effect. At best they really capture the essence of the fruit, especially if you make them using over-ripe fruit.

Before the advent of the freezer, bottling fruits and vegetables in water or sugar syrup was the usual way to preserve them. Now that bottling has become a niche activity and freezing the norm, fruits in syrup have taken on an altogether more luxurious feel. Packed in smart jars and spiced or flavored, they make brilliant presents.

Ginger & lemon nectar

Although not intentionally medicinal, this nectar is soothing and warming and is ideal to drink as a hot beverage if you feel a cold coming on.

Makes about 3 cups (750ml)

2 pieces (50g) of fresh gingerroot, bruised, each about ¾ x 2½ inches

juice and thinly pared zest of 2 lemons

sugar (for quantity see step 2)

1 Place the ginger and lemon zest in a pan with 5 cups (1.2 liters) water. Simmer gently for 40 minutes. Strain through a sieve into a measuring pitcher; discard the zest and ginger.

2 Add the lemon juice to the ginger-infused juice. Add ⅝ cup (400g) sugar for every 1 cup (600ml) liquid and stir over a low heat until all the sugar has dissolved. Bring just to the boil, then quickly remove from the heat.

3 Pour the nectar into clean clip-top or corked bottles and sterilize (see pages 15), or pour into freezer containers, seal, and freeze.

Lemon & orange nectar

A fresh citrus cordial that is so classic and versatile that you can drink it any time. This cordial makes a drink like the best old-fashioned lemonade mixed with orangeade.

Makes about 2 quarts (2 liters)

8–10 lemons

6–8 oranges

3 scant cups (650g) sugar

1 tsp citric acid

1 Pare the rind finely from 1 lemon and 1 orange. Put the sugar, rind, and 2½ cups (600ml) water into a pan. Heat gently to make a syrup, then boil for 5 minutes.

2 Strain through a sieve into a measuring pitcher; discard the zest.

3 Squeeze enough lemons and oranges to produce the same amount of juice as syrup, keeping the same proportions of half lemon, half orange. Mix the syrup and fruit juices together in the pan and add the citric acid, stirring until the powder has dissolved. Bottle as above.

Figs in vanilla syrup

These gorgeous fruits look magnificent in the jar, beautifully pink and jewel-like. Baking the jar in the oven will help the figs to keep.

Makes about 1 pint (500ml)

¼ scant cup (50g) sugar

½ vanilla bean (pod)

approx. 1¼-inch (3cm) piece of cinnamon stick

6 or 7 figs, halved

¼ tsp citric acid

1 Preheat the oven to 300°F (150°C). Place the sugar, vanilla bean, and cinnamon stick in a pan and add 1 cup (220ml) water. Stir over a low heat to dissolve the sugar, then bring to the boil and simmer for 2 minutes to make a syrup. Remove from the heat. Discard the cinnamon stick. Slice the vanilla bean in half lengthwise, scrape out the seeds with a knife, and add them to the syrup.

2 Pack the figs into a clean, sterilized jar (see page 7) with the cut sides facing outward. Push the vanilla bean halves among the figs. Pour the syrup over the figs to fill the jar, swiveling the jar to remove any air bubbles.

3 Wrap aluminum foil over the top of the jar and place it in the oven, on a baking tray lined with several layers of folded newspaper. Bake for 25–30 minutes, by which time the syrup will have turned a lovely shade of pink. Remove from the oven, discard the foil, and seal.

Apricots in syrup

This is a lovely way of using up any luscious apricots that come your way. The syrup is quite spicy and helps make this bottled fruit very special—special enough to serve alone as dessert at the end of a meal. Leaving the whole spices in the jar means it looks good, too.

Makes about 1½ pints (750ml)

1¾ cups (450ml) sugar

pared rind and juice of 1 small orange

1 small cinnamon stick

4 cardamom pods, with seeds crushed

2 star anise

1½ pounds (750g) apricots, halved and stoned

1 Make a syrup by placing 2½ cups (600ml) water in a pan with the sugar, 3 strips of the orange zest plus the juice of the orange, and the spices. Heat gently, stirring to dissolve the sugar before turning up the heat and bringing to a simmer.

2 Add the apricots and poach them until they are cooked but still in whole pieces, then remove them with a slotted spoon and pack them into hot, sterilized jars (see page 7). Bring the syrup to the boil and boil rapidly for 10–15 minutes to thicken and reduce it.

3 Pour the syrup and spices over the fruit to cover completely. Gently tap the jars to release any air bubbles, then seal (see page 11).

NECTARS & CORDIALS

Raspberry nectar

Raspberry nectar makes a lovely alternative to a dollop of jam on rice pudding, for example. Unlike preserves, which often benefit from being made with combinations of flavors, nectars are usually best when made with a single fruit, thus showcasing the individual characteristics of that fruit.

Makes about 2¼ cups (600ml)

4 pints (1kg) overripe raspberries

sugar (for quantity see step 2)

1 Place the raspberries in the top of a double boiler, or in a bowl over a pan of simmering water. Mash the berries with the back of a spoon to break them down and add 1 tablespoon water, then cook until the fruit is soft, the juices are flowing, and the fruit comes to the boil, stirring now and then. Pour into a jelly bag and collect the drips in a measuring pitcher.

2 Add 1 scant ¾ cup (400g) sugar to every 1 cup (600ml) juice and stir over a low heat until all the sugar has dissolved. Bring just to the boil, then quickly remove from the heat.

3 Pour the nectar into clean, clip-top or corked bottles and sterilize (see page 15), or pour into freezer containers, seal, and freeze.

Recipe name

Ingredients

Recipe

Quantity made

Comments

Recipe name

Ingredients

Recipe

Quantity made

Comments

NECTARS & CORDIALS

Recipe name

Ingredients

Recipe

Quantity made

Comments

Recipe name

Ingredients

Recipe

Quantity made

Comments

Recipe name

Ingredients

Recipe

Quantity made

Comments

Recipe name

Ingredients

Recipe

Quantity made

Comments

NECTARS & CORDIALS

Recipe name

Ingredients

Recipe

Quantity made

Comments

Recipe name

Ingredients

Recipe

Quantity made

Comments

Recipe name

Ingredients

Recipe

Quantity made

Comments

Recipe name

Ingredients

Recipe

Quantity made

Comments

NECTARS & CORDIALS

Recipe name

Ingredients

Recipe

Quantity made
Comments

Recipe name

Ingredients

Recipe

Quantity made
Comments

Recipe name

Ingredients

Recipe

Quantity made
Comments

Recipe name

Ingredients

Recipe

Quantity made
Comments

NECTARS & CORDIALS

Recipe name

Ingredients

Recipe

Quantity made

Comments

Recipe name

Ingredients

Recipe

Quantity made

Comments

Recipe name

Ingredients

Recipe name

Ingredients

Recipe

Recipe

Quantity made

Comments

Quantity made

Comments

NECTARS & CORDIALS

Recipe name

Ingredients

Recipe

Quantity made

Comments

Recipe name

Ingredients

Recipe

Quantity made

Comments

Recipe name

Ingredients

Recipe name

Ingredients

Recipe

Recipe

Quantity made

Comments

Quantity made

Comments

NECTARS & CORDIALS

Recipe name

Ingredients

Recipe

Quantity made

Comments

Recipe name

Ingredients

Recipe

Quantity made

Comments

Recipe name

Ingredients

Recipe

Quantity made

Comments

Recipe name

Ingredients

Recipe

Quantity made

Comments

NECTARS & CORDIALS

Recipe name

Ingredients

Recipe

Quantity made

Comments

Recipe name

Ingredients

Recipe

Quantity made

Comments

Recipe name

Ingredients

Recipe

Quantity made

Comments

Recipe name

Ingredients

Recipe

Quantity made

Comments

NECTARS & CORDIALS

Notes

Notes

Notes

Notes

Favorite websites

www.

Notes

Favorite websites

www.

Notes

Favorite websites

www.

Notes

Favorite websites

www.

Notes

Favorite websites

www.

Notes

Favorite websites

www.

Notes

Favorite websites

www.

Notes

Favorite websites

www.

Notes

Favorite websites

www.

Notes

Favorite websites

www.

Notes

Favorite websites
www.
Notes

Favorite websites
www.
Notes

Favorite websites
www.
Notes

Favorite websites
www.
Notes

Favorite websites
www.
Notes

Favorite websites
www.
Notes

Favorite websites
www.
Notes

Favorite websites
www.
Notes

Favorite websites
www.
Notes

Favorite websites
www.
Notes

Useful contacts

Many local hardware stores and well-stocked cook stores sell all the bits and pieces you need for jam making, from preserving pans to jars and labels. Here are a few online companies that also stock the things you will need.

US
www.allamericancanner.com
www.canningparty.com
www.freshpreserving.com

UK
www.lakeland.co.uk
www.waresofknutsford.co.uk
www.justpreserving.co.uk

Jam making resource
www.jamheaven.co.uk

Picture credits
Key: a=above, b=below, r=right, l=left

Gloria Nicol: 5, 6, 7, 8, 9, 11, 12, 13, 14, 16, 17, 20, 22, 24, 47b, 48, 50, 51, 71, 73a, 74, 76, 77, 78, 99, 101, 102, 104, 105

Winfried Heinze: 52, 106

David Mereweather: 10

Lucinda Symonds: 15

www.loupeimages.co.uk: 1, 3, 19, 45, 47a, 73b,